Wraps by the Dozen

Want to create a versatile wardrobe of wraps for yourself, or need a variety of designs for prayer shawls and gifts? Here are 12 simple-to-make choices, from dressy to casual. Our free on-line videos will help you finish with ease!

LEISURE ARTS, INC. • Little Rock, Arkansas

statuesque

 EASY +

Approximate Finished Size:

29" high x 86¾" wide (73.5 cm x 220.5 cm)

SHOPPING LIST

Yarn (Medium Weight)

[3 ounces, 145 yards

(85 grams, 133 meters) per skein]:

☐ 9 skeins

Crochet Hook

☐ Size K (6.5 mm) **or** size needed for gauge

GAUGE INFORMATION

In pattern, one repeat = 4" (10 cm);

   4 rows (Rows 3-6) = 3¼" (8.25 cm)

Gauge Swatch: 6¾" wide x 5¾" high

   (17.25 cm x 14.5 cm)

Ch 20.

Work same as First Half for 6 rows: one dc square and

2 ch-2 sps.

Finish off.

INSTRUCTIONS
FIRST HALF

Ch 210; place a marker in second ch from hook for Second Half placement.

Row 1: Hdc in third ch from hook (**2 skipped chs count as first hdc**) and in each ch across: 209 hdc.

Row 2 (Right side)**:** Ch 3 (**counts as first dc, now and throughout**), turn; dc in next hdc, skip next 2 hdc, (2 dc, ch 2, 2 dc) in next hdc, ★ ch 5, skip next 4 hdc, sc in next hdc, [ch 3, **turn**; 5 dc in next ch-5 sp, ch 3, **turn**; dc in next 4 dc and in next ch (**dc square made**)], skip next 4 hdc, (2 dc, ch 2, 2 dc) in next hdc; repeat from ★ across to last 4 hdc, skip next 2 hdc, dc in last 2 hdc: 20 dc squares and 21 ch-2 sps.

Note: Loop a short piece of yarn around any stitch to mark Row 2 as **right** side.

Row 3: Ch 3, turn; dc in next dc, (2 dc, ch 2, 2 dc) in next ch-2 sp, ★ ch 9, skip next dc square, (2 dc, ch 2, 2 dc) in next ch-2 sp; repeat from ★ across to last 4 dc, skip next 2 dc, dc in last 2 dc: 20 ch-9 sps and 21 ch-2 sps.

Rows 4 and 5: Ch 3, turn; dc in next dc, (2 dc, ch 2, 2 dc) in next ch-2 sp, ★ ch 9, skip next ch-9 sp, (2 dc, ch 2, 2 dc) in next ch-2 sp; repeat from ★ across to last 4 dc, skip next 2 dc, dc in last 2 dc.

Row 6: Ch 3, turn; dc in next dc, (2 dc, ch 2, 2 dc) in next ch-2 sp, ★ ch 5, working **around** ch-9 sps of previous 3 rows, sc in top of turning ch of dc square 4 rows **below**, [ch 3, **turn**; 5 dc in next ch-5 sp, ch 3, **turn**; dc in next 4 dc and in next ch **(dc square made)**], skip next 2 dc, (2 dc, ch 2, 2 dc) in next ch-2 sp; repeat from ★ across to last 4 dc, skip next 2 dc, dc in last 2 dc: 20 dc squares and 21 ch-2 sps.

Rows 7-14: Repeat Rows 3-6 twice: 20 dc squares and 21 ch-2 sps.

Row 15: Ch 3, turn; dc in next dc, (2 dc, ch 2, 2 dc) in next ch-2 sp, ★ ch 4, skip next 7 dc, sc in next ch (top of turning ch), ch 4, (2 dc, ch 2, 2 dc) in next ch-2 sp; repeat from ★ across to last 4 dc, skip next 2 dc, dc in last 2 dc: 40 ch-4 sps and 21 ch-2 sps.

Row 16: Ch 2 **(counts as first hdc, now and throughout)**, turn; hdc in next 3 dc, ★ hdc in next ch-2 sp, skip next 2 dc, hdc in next 4 chs and in next sc, hdc in next 4 chs; repeat from ★ across to last ch-2 sp, hdc in last ch-2 sp and in last 4 dc: 209 hdc.

Finish off.

SECOND HALF

Row 1: With **wrong** side facing and 🎥 working in free loops of beginning ch *(Fig. 1, page 39)*, 👀 join yarn with hdc in first ch *(see Joining With Hdc, page 39)*; hdc in next ch and in each ch across ending in marked ch: 209 hdc.

Rows 2-16: Repeat Rows 2-16 of First Half: 209 hdc.

Do **not** finish off.

EDGING

Rnd 1 (Right side): Ch 2, do **not** turn; 2 hdc in end of each row across short edge; working in sts across long edge, 2 hdc in first hdc, hdc in next hdc and in each hdc across to last hdc, 2 hdc in last hdc; 2 hdc in end of each row across short edge; working in sts across long edge, 2 hdc in first hdc, hdc in next hdc and in each hdc across to last hdc, hdc in last hdc; join with slip st to first hdc: 550 hdc.

Rnd 2: Ch 3, 3 dc in same st as joining, ch 3, **turn**; skip first 3 dc, dc in next dc, ch 3, **turn**; 3 dc in ch-3 sp, skip next 4 hdc on Rnd 1, ★ 4 dc in next hdc, ch 3, **turn**; skip first 3 dc, dc in next dc, ch 3, **turn**; 3 dc in ch-3 sp, skip next 4 hdc on Rnd 1; repeat from ★ around; join with slip st to first dc, finish off.

zesty

Shown on page 7.

 EASY +

Approximate Finished Size:

22" high x 67" wide (56 cm x 170 cm)

SHOPPING LIST

Yarn (Medium Weight)

[3.5 ounces, 170 yards

(100 grams, 156 meters) per skein]:

☐ Orange - 4 skeins

☐ Burnt Orange - 1 skein

Crochet Hook

☐ Size K (6.5 mm) **or** size needed for gauge

GAUGE INFORMATION

In pattern, 2 repeats = 4" (10 cm)

  Rows 1-4 = 3½" (9 cm)

Gauge Swatch: 6" wide x 3½" high

  (15.25 cm x 9 cm)

With Orange, ch 17.

Work same as First Half for 4 rows: 21 dc.

Finish off.

STITCH GUIDE

TREBLE CROCHET *(abbreviated tr)*

YO twice, insert hook in sp indicated, YO and pull up a loop (4 loops on hook), (YO and draw through 2 loops on hook) 3 times.

INSTRUCTIONS
FIRST HALF

With Orange, ch 53; place a marker in fifth ch from hook for Second Half placement.

Row 1: Dc in fifth ch from hook (**4 skipped chs count as first dc plus ch 2**), ch 2, ★ skip next 5 chs, (dc, ch 2) twice in next ch; repeat from ★ across to last 6 chs, skip next 5 chs, (dc, ch 2, dc) in last ch: 17 ch-2 sps.

Row 2 (Right side)**:** Turn; slip st in first ch-2 sp, ch 3 (**counts as first dc, now and throughout**), 6 dc in same sp, ★ skip next ch-2 sp, 7 dc in next ch-2 sp; repeat from ★ across: 63 dc.

Note: Loop a short piece of yarn around any stitch to mark Row 2 as **right** side.

Row 3: Turn; slip st in first 4 dc, ch 5 **(counts as first dc plus ch 2, now and throughout)**, dc in same st as last slip st made, ★ ch 2, skip next 6 dc, (dc, ch 2, dc) in next dc; repeat from ★ across to last 3 dc, leave last 3 dc unworked: 17 ch-2 sps.

Row 4: Turn; slip st in first ch-2 sp, ch 3, 6 dc in same sp, ★ skip next ch-2 sp, 7 dc in next ch-2 sp; repeat from ★ across: 63 dc.

Rows 5-36: Repeat Rows 3 and 4, 16 times: 63 dc.

Finish off.

SECOND HALF

Row 1: With **wrong** side facing and working in free loops of beginning ch *(Fig. 1, page 39)*, join Orange with slip st in first ch; ch 5, dc in same st, ch 2, ★ skip next 5 chs, (dc, ch 2) twice in next ch; repeat from ★ across to within 5 chs of marked ch, skip next 5 chs, (dc, ch 2, dc) in marked ch; do **not** remove marker: 17 ch-2 sps.

Rows 2-36: Repeat Rows 2-36 of First Half: 63 dc.

Do **not** finish off.

EDGING

Rnd 1 (Right side)**:** Ch 1, do **not** turn; working in end of rows, sc in top of first dc on Row 36, ch 4, skip next row, [sc in top of first dc on next row, ch 4, skip next row] 17 times, dc in marked ch of beginning ch, † [ch 4, skip next row, sc in top of first dc on next row] 18 times; working in sts across Row 36, ch 3, skip next 2 dc, sc in next dc (center dc of 7-dc group), ch 3, ★ skip next 3 dc, sc in sp **before** next dc *(Fig. 2, page 39)*, ch 3, skip next 3 dc, sc in next dc, ch 3; repeat from ★ across to last 3 dc, skip next 2 dc †, sc in last dc, ch 4; working in end of rows, skip first 2 rows, [sc in top of first dc on next row, ch 4, skip next row] 17 times, dc in first ch of beginning ch, repeat from † to † once; join with slip st to first sc, finish off: 108 sts and 108 sps.

Rnd 2: With **right** side facing, join Burnt Orange with sc in same st as joining *(see Joining With Sc, page 39)*; † ch 5, [skip next ch-4 sp, sc in next st, ch 5] 36 times, skip next ch-3 sp, sc in next sc, [ch 7, skip next 2 ch-3 sps, sc in next sc] 8 times, ch 5, skip next ch-3 sp †, sc in next sc, repeat from † to † once; join with slip st to first sc: 92 sc and 92 sps.

Rnd 3: Ch 5, dc in same st as joining, ch 3, skip next sp, ★ (dc, ch 2, dc) in next sc, ch 3, skip next sp; repeat from ★ around; join with slip st to first dc: 184 sps.

Rnd 4: (Slip st, ch 1, sc) in next ch-2 sp, (hdc, dc, tr, dc, hdc) in next ch-3 sp, ★ sc in next ch-2 sp, (hdc, dc, tr, dc, hdc) in next ch-3 sp; repeat from ★ around; join with slip st to first sc, finish off.

charming

 EASY

Approximate Finished Size:

16" high x 68" wide (40.5 cm x 172.5 cm)

SHOPPING LIST

Yarn (Medium Weight)

[3.5 ounces, 170 yards

(100 grams, 156 meters) per skein]:

☐ Green - 2 skeins

☐ Yellow - 2 skeins

Crochet Hook

☐ Size K (6.5 mm) **or** size needed for gauge

GAUGE INFORMATION

In pattern, 2 repeats = 5¾" (14.5 cm);

6 rows (Rows 3-8) = 4" (10 cm)

Gauge Swatch: 5¾" wide x 4" high

(14.5 cm x 10 cm)

With Green, ch 25.

Work same as First Half for 6 rows: 16 sts and 4 ch-3 sps.

Finish off.

STITCH GUIDE

TREBLE CROCHET *(abbreviated tr)*

★ YO twice, insert hook in st or sp indicated, YO and pull up a loop (4 loops on hook), (YO and draw through 2 loops on hook) 3 times.

INSTRUCTIONS

FIRST HALF

With Green, ch 55; place a marker in fourth ch from hook for Second Half placement.

Row 1: Sc in seventh ch from hook (**6 skipped chs count as first hdc plus ch 2 and 2 skipped chs**), ★ ch 5, skip next 4 chs, sc in next ch; repeat from ★ across to last 3 chs, ch 2, skip next 2 chs, hdc in last ch: 12 sts and 11 sps.

Row 2 (Right side)**:** Ch 3 (**counts as first dc, now and throughout**), turn; 3 dc in next ch-2 sp, ch 2, sc in next ch-5 sp, ch 2, ★ (3 dc, ch 2) twice in next ch-5 sp, sc in next ch-5 sp, ch 2; repeat from ★ across to last ch-2 sp, 3 dc in last ch-2 sp, dc in last hdc; finish off: 37 sts and 14 ch-2 sps.

Note: Loop a short piece of yarn around any stitch to mark Row 2 as **right** side.

Row 3: With **wrong** side facing, 🎥 join Yellow with sc in first dc *(see Joining With Sc, page 39)*; ch 3, dc in next 3 dc, skip next 2 ch-2 sps, dc in next 3 dc, ch 3, ★ sc in next ch-2 sp, ch 3, dc in next 3 dc, skip next 2 ch-2 sps, dc in next 3 dc, ch 3; repeat from ★ across to last dc, sc in last dc: 36 sts and 10 ch-3 sps.

Row 4: Ch 5 **(counts as first dc plus ch 2, now and throughout)**, turn; skip next ch-3 sp, sc in next dc, ch 5, skip next 4 dc, sc in next dc, ★ ch 5, skip next 2 ch-3 sps, sc in next dc, ch 5, skip next 4 dc, sc in next dc; repeat from ★ across to last ch-3 sp, ch 2, skip last ch-3 sp, dc in last sc: 12 sts and 11 sps.

Row 5: Ch 1, turn; sc in first dc, skip next ch-2 sp, (3 dc, ch 2, 3 dc) in next ch-5 sp, ★ ch 2, sc in next ch-5 sp, ch 2, (3 dc, ch 2, 3 dc) in next ch-5 sp; repeat from ★ across to last ch-2 sp, skip last ch-2 sp, sc in last dc; finish off: 36 sts and 13 ch-2 sps.

Row 6: With **right** side facing, 🎥 join Green with dc in first sc *(see Joining With Dc, page 39)*; dc in next 3 dc, ch 3, sc in next ch-2 sp, ch 3, dc in next 3 dc, ★ skip next 2 ch-2 sps, dc in next 3 dc, ch 3, sc in next ch-2 sp, ch 3, dc in next 3 dc; repeat from ★ across to last sc, dc in last sc: 37 sts and 10 ch-3 sps.

Row 7: Ch 5, turn; skip first 3 dc, sc in next dc, ch 5, skip next 2 ch-3 sps, sc in next dc, ★ ch 5, skip next 4 dc, sc in next dc, ch 5, skip next 2 ch-3 sps, sc in next dc; repeat from ★ across to last 3 dc, ch 2, skip next 2 dc, dc in last dc: 12 sts and 11 sps.

Row 8: Ch 3, turn; 3 dc in next ch-2 sp, ch 2, sc in next ch-5 sp, ch 2, ★ (3 dc, ch 2) twice in next ch-5 sp, sc in next ch-5 sp, ch 2; repeat from ★ across to last ch-2 sp, 3 dc in last ch-2 sp, dc in last dc; finish off: 37 sts and 14 ch-2 sps.

Rows 9-49: Repeat Rows 3-8, 6 times; then repeat Rows 3-7 once **more**: 12 sts and 11 sps.

Finish off.

SECOND HALF

Row 1: With **wrong** side facing and 🎥 working in free loops of beginning ch *(Fig. 1, page 39)*, 🎥 join Green with hdc in first ch *(see Joining With Hdc, page 39)*; ch 2, skip next 2 chs, sc in next ch, ★ ch 5, skip next 4 chs, sc in next ch; repeat from ★ across to within 2 chs of marked ch, ch 2, skip next 2 chs, hdc in marked ch; do **not** remove marker: 12 sts and 11 sps.

Rows 2-49: Repeat Rows 2-49 of First Half: 12 sts and 11 sps.

Do **not** finish off.

EDGING

Rnd 1 (Right side)**:** Turn; slip st in next ch-2 sp, ch 4 **(counts as first tr)**, (2 tr, 3 dc) in same sp, ♥ hdc in next sc, 5 sc in next ch-5 sp, hdc in next sc, [7 dc in next ch-5 sp, hdc in next sc, 5 sc in next ch-5 sp, hdc in next sc] 4 times, (3 dc, 3 tr, 3 dc) in last sp; working in end of rows, (hdc, sc) in next dc row, † skip next sc row, 2 sc in next dc row, skip next sc row, [(sc, hdc) in next dc row, 7 dc in next dc row, (hdc, sc) in next dc row, skip next sc row, 2 sc in next dc row, skip next sc row] 7 times †, (sc, hdc, 2 dc) in next dc row, 3 dc in next hdc row, 3 tr in marked ch, 3 dc in next hdc row, (2 dc, hdc, sc) in next dc row, repeat from † to † once, (sc, hdc) in next dc row ♥, (3 dc, 3 tr, 3 dc) in next sp, repeat from ♥ to ♥ once, 3 dc in same sp as first tr; join with slip st to first tr, finish off.

passionate

Shown on page 13.

 EASY

Approximate Finished Size:

22¼" high x 66" wide (56.5 cm x 167.5 cm)

SHOPPING LIST

Yarn (Medium Weight)

[3.5 ounces, 170 yards

(100 grams, 156 meters) per skein]:

☐ 7 skeins

Crochet Hook

☐ Size J (6 mm) **or** size needed for gauge

GAUGE INFORMATION

In pattern, 2 repeats (12 dc) = 4" (10 cm)

Rows 1-6 = 4¾" (12 cm)

Gauge Swatch: 6¼" wide x 4¾" high

(16 cm x 12 cm)

Ch 21.

Work same as First Half for 6 rows: 19 dc.

Finish off.

INSTRUCTIONS

FIRST HALF

Ch 51; place a marker in third ch from hook for Second Half placement.

Row 1 (Right side)**:** 5 Dc in sixth ch from hook (**5 skipped chs count as first dc plus 2 skipped chs**), skip next 2 chs, dc in next ch, ★ skip next 2 chs, 5 dc in next ch, skip next 2 chs, dc in next ch; repeat from ★ across: 49 dc.

Note: Loop a short piece of yarn around any stitch to mark Row 1 as **right** side.

Rows 2-38: Ch 3 (**counts as first dc, now and throughout**), turn; ★ skip next 2 dc, 5 dc in next dc, skip next 2 dc, dc in next dc; repeat from ★ across.

Finish off.

SECOND HALF

Row 1: With **right** side facing and working in free loops of beginning ch *(Fig. 1, page 39)*, join yarn with dc in first ch *(see Joining With Dc, page 39)*; ★ skip next 2 chs, 5 dc in next ch, skip next 2 chs, dc in next ch; repeat from ★ across ending in marked ch: 49 dc.

Rnd 2: Ch 2, do **not** turn; (hdc, ch 3, 2 hdc) in same st as joining, ch 3, † skip next 2 hdc, (hdc in next hdc, ch 3, skip next 2 hdc) 16 times, (2 hdc, ch 3) twice in next hdc, skip next 2 hdc, (hdc in next hdc, ch 3, skip next 2 hdc) 49 times †, (2 hdc, ch 3) twice in next hdc, repeat from † to † once; join with slip st to first hdc: 146 hdc and 138 ch-3 sps.

Rnd 3: Slip st in next hdc and in next ch-3 sp, ch 3, 6 dc in same sp, ★ † sc in next ch-3 sp, ch 3, sc in next ch-3 sp, (5 dc in next ch-3 sp, sc in next ch-3 sp, ch 3, sc in next ch-3 sp) across to next corner ch-3 sp †, 7 dc in corner sp; repeat from ★ 2 times **more**, then repeat from † to † once; join with slip st to first dc: 238 dc and 46 ch-3 sps.

Rnd 4: Ch 4 **(counts as first dc plus ch 1)**, dc in next dc, (ch 1, dc in next dc) 5 times, ★ † ch 2, sc in next ch-3 sp, ch 2, [skip next sc, dc in next dc, (ch 1, dc in next dc) 4 times, ch 2, sc in next ch-3 sp, ch 2] across to within one sc of next corner 7-dc group, skip next sc †, dc in next dc, (ch 1, dc in next dc) 6 times; repeat from ★ 2 times **more**, then repeat from † to † once; join with slip st to first dc: 192 ch-1 sps and 92 ch-2 sps.

Rnd 5: (Slip st, ch 3, 2 dc) in next ch-1 sp, 3 dc in each of next 5 ch-1 sps, † skip next ch-2 sp, sc in next sc, skip next ch-2 sp, [3 dc in each of next 4 ch-1 sps, skip next ch-2 sp, sc in next sc, skip next ch-2 sp] 5 times, 3 dc in each of next 6 ch-1 sps, skip next ch-2 sp, sc in next sc, skip next ch-2 sp, [3 dc in each of next 4 ch-1 sps, skip next ch-2 sp, sc in next sc, skip next ch-2 sp] 16 times †, 3 dc in each of next 6 ch-1 sps, repeat from † to † once; join with slip st to first dc, finish off.

Rows 2-38: Repeat Rows 2-38 of First Half: 49 dc.

Do **not** finish off.

EDGING

Rnd 1 (Right side)**:** Ch 2 **(counts as first hdc, now and throughout)**, turn; 2 hdc in same dc, † hdc in next dc and in each dc across to last dc, 3 hdc in last dc; working in end of rows, 2 hdc in each of first 8 rows, (hdc in next row, 2 hdc in each of next 9 rows) 3 times, hdc in beginning ch, (2 hdc in each of next 9 rows, hdc in next row) 3 times, 2 hdc in each of last 8 rows †, working in sts across Row 38, 4 hdc in first dc, repeat from † to † once, hdc in same st as first hdc; join with slip st to first hdc: 402 hdc.

frolic

■■□□ **EASY +**

Approximate Finished Size:

20" high x 73½" wide (51 cm x 186.5 cm)

SHOPPING LIST

Yarn (Medium Weight)

[3 ounces, 145 yards

(85 grams, 133 meters) per skein]:

☐ 6 skeins

Crochet Hook

☐ Size J (6 mm) **or** size needed for gauge

Additional Supplies

☐ Yarn needle

GAUGE INFORMATION

In pattern, one repeat

(from point to point) = 5" (12.75 cm);

6 rows = 5¼" (13.25 cm)

Gauge Swatch: 10" wide x 5½" high

(25.5 cm x 14 cm)

Ch 36.

Work same as First Half for 6 rows: 25 sts and 16 sps.

Finish off.

STITCH GUIDE

DOUBLE CROCHET 3 TOGETHER

(abbreviated dc3tog) (uses next 3 sts)

★ YO, insert hook in **next** st, YO and pull up a loop, YO and draw through 2 loops on hook; repeat from ★ 2 times **more**, YO and draw through all 4 loops on hook.

DOUBLE CROCHET 5 TOGETHER

(abbreviated dc5tog) (uses next 5 sts)

YO, insert hook in next dc, YO and pull up a loop, YO and draw through 2 loops on hook, ★ YO, skip **next** ch, insert hook in **next** st, YO and pull up a loop, YO and draw through 2 loops on hook; repeat from ★ once **more**, YO and draw through all 4 loops on hook.

CLUSTER (uses next 5 sts)

YO, insert hook in next st, YO and pull up a loop, YO and draw through 2 loops on hook, YO twice, skip next ch, insert hook in next st, YO and pull up a loop, (YO and draw through 2 loops on hook) twice, [YO twice, insert hook in **same** st, YO and pull up a loop, (YO and draw through 2 loops on hook) twice] 3 times, YO, skip next ch, insert hook in next st, YO and pull up a loop, YO and draw through 2 loops on hook, YO and draw through all 7 loops on hook.

INSTRUCTIONS
FIRST HALF

Ch 72; place a marker in second ch from hook for Second Half placement.

Row 1 (Right side)**:** Dc in fourth ch from hook, ch 1, skip next ch, (dc in next ch, ch 1, skip next ch) twice, (3 dc, ch 3, 3 dc) in next ch, ch 1, skip next ch, ★ (dc in next ch, ch 1, skip next ch) 3 times, dc3tog, ch 1, skip next ch, (dc in next ch, ch 1, skip next ch) 3 times, (3 dc, ch 3, 3 dc) in next ch, ch 1, skip next ch; repeat from ★ 2 times **more**, (dc in next ch, ch 1, skip next ch) twice, dc3tog: 51 sts and 34 sps.

Note: Loop a short piece of yarn around any stitch to mark Row 1 as **right** side.

Row 2: Ch 2, turn; (skip next ch, dc in next dc, ch 1) 3 times, (3 dc, ch 3, 3 dc) in next ch-3 sp, ch 1, skip next 2 dc, ★ (dc in next dc, ch 1, skip next ch) 3 times, work Cluster, ch 1, (skip next ch, dc in next dc, ch 1) 3 times, (3 dc, ch 3, 3 dc) in next ch-3 sp, ch 1, skip next 2 dc; repeat from ★ 2 times **more**, (dc in next dc, ch 1, skip next ch) twice, dc3tog.

Row 3: Ch 2, turn; (skip next ch, dc in next dc, ch 1) 3 times, (3 dc, ch 3, 3 dc) in next ch-3 sp, ch 1, skip next 2 dc, ★ (dc in next dc, ch 1, skip next ch) 3 times, dc5tog, ch 1, (skip next ch, dc in next dc, ch 1) 3 times, (3 dc, ch 3, 3 dc) in next ch-3 sp, ch 1, skip next 2 dc; repeat from ★ 2 times **more**, (dc in next dc, ch 1, skip next ch) twice, dc3tog.

Rows 4-40: Repeat Rows 2 and 3, 18 times; then repeat Row 2 once **more**.

Finish off.

SECOND HALF

Foundation Row: With **wrong** side facing and 🎥 working in free loops of beginning ch *(Fig. 1, page 39)*, join yarn with slip st in marked ch, do **not** remove marker; ch 16, skip next 16 chs, slip st in next ch, ★ ch 17, skip next 17 chs, slip st in next ch; repeat from ★ once **more**, ch 16, skip next 16 chs, slip st in last ch: 66 chs and 5 slip sts.

Row 1 (Right side)**:** Ch 2, turn; working in slip sts and chs, skip first slip st and next ch, (dc in next ch, ch 1, skip next ch) 3 times, (3 dc, ch 3, 3 dc) in next ch, ch 1, skip next ch, ★ (dc in next ch, ch 1, skip next ch) 3 times, dc3tog, ch 1, skip next ch, (dc in next ch, ch 1, skip next ch) 3 times, (3 dc, ch 3, 3 dc) in next ch, ch 1, skip next ch; repeat from ★ 2 times **more**, (dc in next ch, ch 1, skip next ch) twice, dc3tog: 51 sts and 34 sps.

Rows 2-40: Repeat Rows 2-40 of First Half.

Do **not** finish off.

EDGING

Rnd 1 (Right side)**:** Turn; ★ slip st **loosely** in each st across Row 40; sc evenly across end of rows; repeat from ★ once **more**; join with slip st to first slip st, finish off.

DIAMOND TRIM

FIRST DIAMOND

Rnd 1: With **wrong** side facing and working in free loops of beginning ch, join yarn with slip st in the slip st in marked ch on First Half of diamond opening; slip st in next 5 chs, work Cluster, slip st in next 6 chs and in next slip st, slip st in next 6 chs, work Cluster, slip st in last 5 chs; join with slip st to first slip st, finish off.

SECOND & THIRD DIAMONDS

Rnd 1: With **wrong** side facing and working in free loops of beginning ch, join yarn with slip st in either slip st on Second Half of diamond opening; slip st in next 6 chs, work Cluster, slip st in next 6 chs and in next slip st, slip st in next 6 chs, work Cluster, slip st in last 6 chs; join with slip st to first slip st, finish off.

LAST DIAMOND

Rnd 1: With **wrong** side facing and working in free loops of beginning ch, join yarn with slip st in last slip st on Second Half of diamond opening; slip st in next 5 chs, work Cluster, slip st in next 6 chs and in next slip st, slip st in next 6 chs, work Cluster, slip st in last 5 chs; join with slip st to first slip st, finish off.

Optional Bows: Cut eight 12" (30.5 cm) strands of yarn. Lay Shawl on a flat surface. Thread yarn needle with 2 strands of yarn held together and sew through ch at base of (3 dc, ch 3, 3 dc) on each side of center. Tie a knot, then tie ends into a bow; trim ends. Repeat for remaining 3 Bows.

COZY

 EASY +

Approximate Finished Size:

24" high x 78¾" wide (61 cm x 200 cm)

SHOPPING LIST

Yarn (Medium Weight)

[3 ounces, 145 yards

(85 grams, 133 meters) per skein]:

☐ Lt Green - 3 skeins

[3.5 ounces, 170 yards

(100 grams, 156 meters) per skein]:

☐ Green - 3 skeins

☐ Dk Green - 3 skeins

Crochet Hook

☐ Size I (5.5 mm) **or** size needed for gauge

Additional Supplies

☐ Yarn needle

GAUGE INFORMATION

In pattern, one repeat

(from point to point) = 5¾" (14.5 cm);

5 rows = 4¼" (10.75 cm)

One Granny Square = 3¾" (9.5 cm)

Gauge Swatch: 11¾" wide x 3½" high

(30 cm x 9 cm)

With Lt Green, ch 50.

Work same as First Half for 4 rows: 44 dc, 2 Clusters, and

2 ch-3 sps.

STITCH GUIDE

🎥 **CLUSTER** (uses one st or sp)

★ YO, insert hook in st or sp indicated, YO and pull up a

loop, YO and draw through 2 loops on hook; repeat from ★

2 times **more**, YO and draw through all 4 loops on hook.

INSTRUCTIONS
FIRST HALF

With Lt Green, ch 96; place a marker in third ch from hook

for Second Half placement.

Row 1 (Right side): 3 Dc in sixth ch from hook **(5 skipped chs count as first dc plus 2 skipped chs)**, skip next 2 chs, (3 dc in next ch, skip next 2 chs) twice, (3 dc, ch 3, 3 dc) in next ch, skip next 2 chs, ★ (3 dc in next ch, skip next 2 chs) twice, work Cluster in next ch, skip next 4 chs, work Cluster in next ch, skip next 2 chs, (3 dc in next ch, skip next 2 chs) twice, (3 dc, ch 3, 3 dc) in next ch, skip next 2 chs; repeat from ★ 2 times **more**, (3 dc in next ch, skip next 2 chs) 3 times, dc in last ch: 80 dc, 6 Clusters, and 4 ch-3 sps.

Note: Loop a short piece of yarn around any stitch to mark Row 1 as **right** side.

Rows 2 and 3: Ch 3 **(counts as first dc, now and throughout)**, turn; [skip next 3 dc,  3 dc in sp **before** next dc *(Fig. 2, page 39)*] 3 times, (3 dc, ch 3, 3 dc) in next ch-3 sp, skip next 3 dc, ★ (3 dc in sp **before** next dc, skip next 3 dc) twice, work Cluster in sp **before** next Cluster, skip next 2 Clusters, work Cluster in sp **before** next dc, (skip next 3 dc, 3 dc in sp **before** next dc) twice, (3 dc, ch 3, 3 dc) in next ch-3 sp, skip next 3 dc; repeat from ★ 2 times **more**, (3 dc in sp **before** next dc, skip next 3 dc) 3 times, dc in last dc.

Row 4: Ch 3, turn; (skip next 3 dc, 3 dc in sp **before** next dc) 3 times, (3 dc, ch 3, 3 dc) in next ch-3 sp, skip next 3 dc, ★ (3 dc in sp **before** next dc, skip next 3 dc) twice, work Cluster in sp **before** next Cluster, skip next 2 Clusters, work Cluster in sp **before** next dc, (skip next 3 dc, 3 dc in sp **before** next dc) twice, (3 dc, ch 3, 3 dc) in next ch-3 sp, skip next 3 dc; repeat from ★ 2 times **more**, (3 dc in sp **before** next dc, skip next 3 dc) 3 times, dc in last dc; finish off.

Row 5: With **right** side facing,  join Green with dc in first dc *(see Joining With Dc, page 39)*; (skip next 3 dc, 3 dc in sp **before** next dc) 3 times, (3 dc, ch 3, 3 dc) in next ch-3 sp, skip next 3 dc, ★ (3 dc in sp **before** next dc, skip next 3 dc) twice, work Cluster in sp **before** next Cluster, skip next 2 Clusters, work Cluster in sp **before** next dc, (skip next 3 dc, 3 dc in sp **before** next dc) twice, (3 dc, ch 3, 3 dc) in next ch-3 sp, skip next 3 dc; repeat from ★ 2 times **more**, (3 dc in sp **before** next dc, skip next 3 dc) 3 times, dc in last dc.

Row 6: Ch 3, turn; (skip next 3 dc, 3 dc in sp **before** next dc) 3 times, (3 dc, ch 3, 3 dc) in next ch-3 sp, skip next 3 dc, ★ (3 dc in sp **before** next dc, skip next 3 dc) twice, work Cluster in sp **before** next Cluster, skip next 2 Clusters, work Cluster in sp **before** next dc, (skip next 3 dc, 3 dc in sp **before** next dc) twice, (3 dc, ch 3, 3 dc) in next ch-3 sp, skip next 3 dc; repeat from ★ 2 times **more**, (3 dc in sp **before** next dc, skip next 3 dc) 3 times, dc in last dc; finish off.

Rows 7 and 8: With Dk Green, repeat Rows 5 and 6.

Rows 9 and 10: Repeat Rows 5 and 6.

Row 11: With **right** side facing, join Lt Green with dc in first dc; (skip next 3 dc, 3 dc in sp **before** next dc) 3 times, (3 dc, ch 3, 3 dc) in next ch-3 sp, skip next 3 dc, ★ (3 dc in sp **before** next dc, skip next 3 dc) twice, work Cluster in sp **before** next Cluster, skip next 2 Clusters, work Cluster in sp **before** next dc, (skip next 3 dc, 3 dc in sp **before** next dc) twice, (3 dc, ch 3, 3 dc) in next ch-3 sp, skip next 3 dc; repeat from ★ 2 times **more**, (3 dc in sp **before** next dc, skip next 3 dc) 3 times, dc in last dc.

Rows 12-44: Repeat Rows 2-11, 3 times; then repeat Rows 2-4 once **more**.

SECOND HALF

Foundation Row: With **wrong** side facing and working in sps and in free loops of beginning ch *(Fig. 1, page 39)*, join Lt Green with sc in marked ch *(see Joining With Sc, page 39)*; ch 23, skip next 7 ch-2 sps, ★ sc in next ch-4 sp, ch 23, skip next 7 ch-2 sps; repeat from ★ 2 times **more**, sc in last ch: 92 chs and 5 sc.

Row 1 (Right side)**:** Ch 3, turn; skip next 2 chs, (3 dc in next ch, skip next 2 chs) 3 times, (3 dc, ch 3, 3 dc) in next ch, skip next 2 chs, ★ (3 dc in next ch, skip next 2 chs) twice, work Cluster in next ch, skip next 5 sts (4 chs and one sc), work Cluster in next ch, skip next 2 chs, (3 dc in next ch, skip next 2 chs) twice, (3 dc, ch 3, 3 dc) in next ch, skip next 2 chs; repeat from ★ 2 times **more**, (3 dc in next ch, skip next 2 chs) 3 times, dc in last sc: 80 dc, 6 Clusters, and 4 ch-3 sps.

Rows 2-44: Repeat Rows 2-44 of First Half.

GRANNY SQUARE (Make 4)

With Dk Green, ch 6; join with slip st to form a ring.

Rnd 1 (Right side)**:** Ch 3, 2 dc in ring, ch 2, (3 dc in ring, ch 2) 3 times; join with slip st to first dc, finish off: 12 dc and 4 ch-2 sps.

Note: Mark Rnd 1 as **right** side.

Rnd 2: With **right** side facing, join Green with dc any ch-2 sp; (2 dc, ch 2, 3 dc) in same ch-2 sp, ch 1, ★ (3 dc, ch 2, 3 dc) in next ch-2 sp, ch 1; repeat from ★ 2 times **more**; join with slip st to first dc, finish off: 24 dc and 8 sps.

Rnd 3: With **right** side facing, join Dk Green with dc in any corner ch-2 sp; (2 dc, ch 2, 3 dc) in same sp, ch 1, 3 dc in next ch-1 sp, ch 1, ★ (3 dc, ch 2, 3 dc) in next corner ch-2 sp, ch 1, 3 dc in next ch-1 sp, ch 1; repeat from ★ 2 times **more**; join with slip st to first dc, finish off.

With **right** sides of Shawl and Granny Squares facing and using Dk Green, sew one Granny Square into each space formed between First and Second Halves.

EDGING

With **right** side of long edge facing and working in end of rows, join Dk Green with dc in first row; † dc evenly across (approximately 2 or 3 dc per row) ending in last row; working across sts on Row 44, skip first 4 dc, (3 dc in sp **before** next dc, skip next 3 dc) 3 times, 6 dc in next ch-3 sp, (skip next 3 dc, 3 dc in sp **before** next st) 3 times, [skip next 2 Clusters, (3 dc in sp **before** next dc, skip next 3 dc) 3 times, 6 dc in next ch-3 sp, (skip next 3 dc, 3 dc in sp **before** next st) 3 times] 3 times, skip next 3 dc †; working in end of rows, repeat from † to † once; join with slip st to first dc, finish off.

romance

Approximate Finished Size:

25" wide x 63" high (63.5 cm x 160 cm)

SHOPPING LIST

Yarn (Medium Weight)

[3.5 ounces, 170 yards

(100 grams, 156 meters) per skein]:

☐ 5 skeins

Crochet Hook

☐ Size K (6.5 mm) **or** size needed for gauge

GAUGE INFORMATION

In pattern, two repeats (14 sts) = 4" (10 cm);

4 rows = 3" (7.5 cm)

Gauge Swatch: 4½" wide x 3" high

(11.5 cm x 7.5 cm)

Ch 17.

Work same as First Half for 4 rows: 12 dc and 2 ch-2 sps.
Finish off.

——— STITCH GUIDE ———

🎥 **TREBLE CROCHET** *(abbreviated tr)*

YO twice, insert hook in sp indicated, YO and pull up a
loop (4 loops on hook), (YO and draw through 2 loops on
hook) 3 times.

🎥 **DOUBLE TREBLE CROCHET** *(abbreviated dtr)*

YO 3 times, insert hook in sp indicated, YO and pull up a
loop (5 loops on hook), (YO and draw through 2 loops on
hook) 4 times.

🎥 **CROSS ST** (uses next 4 sts)

Skip next 3 sts, dc in next st, ch 2, working **around** dc just
made, dc in center skipped st.

INSTRUCTIONS
FIRST HALF

Ch 185; place a marker in third ch from hook for
Second Half placement.

Row 1 (Right side)**:** Dc in seventh ch from hook (**6 skipped
chs count as first dc plus 3 skipped chs**), ch 2, working
around dc just made, dc in fifth skipped ch, skip next ch,
3 dc in next ch, ★ work Cross St, skip next ch, 3 dc in next
ch; repeat from ★ across to last 2 chs, skip next ch, dc in
last ch: 152 dc and 30 ch-2 sps.

Note: Loop a short piece of yarn around any stitch to mark Row 1 as **right** side.

Rows 2-15: Ch 3 (**counts as first dc, now and throughout**), turn; skip next 2 dc, dc in next dc, ch 1, working **around** dc just made, dc in first skipped dc, 3 dc in next ch-2 sp, (work Cross St, 3 dc in next ch-2 sp) across to last 2 dc, skip next dc, dc in last dc.

Finish off.

SECOND HALF

Row 1: With **right** side facing and working in sps and 🎥 in free loops of beginning ch (*Fig. 1, page 39*), 🎥 join yarn with dc in first ch (*see Joining With Dc, page 39*); skip next 2 chs, dc in next ch, ch 2, working **around** dc just made, dc in first skipped ch, 3 dc in next sp (between dc of Cross St on First Half), ★ skip next 3 chs, dc in next ch, ch 2, working **around** dc just made, dc in center skipped ch, 3 dc in next sp (between dc of Cross St on First Half); repeat from ★ across to within 2 chs of marked ch, skip next 2 chs, dc in marked ch: 152 dc and 30 ch-2 sps.

Rows 2-15: Repeat Rows 2-15 of First Half.

Do **not** finish off.

EDGING

Rnd 1 (Right side)**:** Ch 2 (**counts as first hdc**), do **not** turn; working in end of rows, hdc in first row, ch 2, † (skip next row, 2 hdc in next row, ch 2) 14 times, (2 hdc, ch 2) twice in last row, ch 2; working in sts across Row 15, skip next 2 dc, 🎥 2 hdc in sp **before** next dc (*Fig. 2, page 39*), ch 2, ★ skip next 3 dc, 2 hdc in sp **before** next dc, ch 2, skip next 2 dc, 2 hdc in sp **before** next dc, ch 2; repeat from ★ across to last 4 dc, skip last 4 dc †; working in end of rows, (2 hdc, ch 2) twice in first row, repeat from † to † once, 2 hdc in end of same row as first hdc, ch 1, sc in first hdc to form last ch-2 sp: 308 hdc and 154 ch-2 sps.

Rnd 2: Ch 3, do **not** turn; 4 dc in last ch-2 sp made, † sc in next ch-2 sp, (7 dc in next ch-2 sp, sc in next ch-2 sp) 7 times, 9 dc in next ch-2 sp, sc in next ch-2 sp, (7 dc in next ch-2 sp, sc in next ch-2 sp) 14 times, 5 tr in next ch-2 sp, skip next hdc, 3 dtr in sp **before** next hdc, 5 tr in next ch-2 sp, sc in next ch-2 sp, (7 dc in next ch-2 sp, sc in next ch-2 sp) 14 times †, 9 dc in next ch-2 sp, repeat from † to † once, 4 dc in same sp as first dc; join with slip st to first dc, finish off.

joy

 EASY +

Approximate Finished Size:

19½" high x 66" wide (49.5 cm x 167.5 cm)

SHOPPING LIST

Yarn (Medium Weight)

[3.5 ounces, 170 yards
(100 grams, 156 meters) per skein]:

☐ 5 skeins

Crochet Hook

☐ Size J (6 mm) **or** size needed for gauge

GAUGE INFORMATION

In pattern, one repeat = 3½" (9 cm);
   3 rows = 2¼" (5.75 cm)

Gauge Swatch: 7" wide x 2¼" high
   (17.75 cm x 5.75 cm)

Ch 28.

Work same as First Half for 3 rows: 11 dc and 8 ch-2 sps.

Finish off.

INSTRUCTIONS
FIRST HALF

Ch 64; place a marker in fourth ch from hook for Second Half placement.

Row 1: 2 Dc in fourth ch from hook (**3 skipped chs count as first dc**), ch 2, skip next 3 chs, sc in next ch, ch 5, skip next 3 chs, sc in next ch, ★ ch 2, skip next 3 chs, 5 dc in next ch, ch 2, skip next 3 chs, sc in next ch, ch 5, skip next 3 chs, sc in next ch; repeat from ★ across to last 4 chs, ch 2, skip next 3 chs, 3 dc in last ch: 36 sts and 15 sps.

Row 2 (Right side)**:** Ch 4 (**counts as first dc plus ch 1, now and throughout**), turn; dc in next dc, ch 1, dc in next dc, ch 2, skip next ch-2 sp, sc in next ch-5 sp, ch 2, skip next ch-2 sp, dc in next dc, ★ (ch 1, dc in next dc) 4 times, ch 2, skip next ch-2 sp, sc in next ch-5 sp, ch 2, skip next ch-2 sp, dc in next dc; repeat from ★ across to last 2 dc, (ch 1, dc in next dc) twice: 31 sts and 30 sps.

Note: Loop a short piece of yarn around any stitch to mark Row 2 as **right** side.

Row 3: Ch 5 (**counts as first dc plus ch 2**), turn; dc in next dc, ch 2, dc in next dc, skip next 2 ch-2 sps, dc in next dc, ★ (ch 2, dc in next dc) 4 times, skip next 2 ch-2 sps, dc in next dc; repeat from ★ across to last 2 dc, (ch 2, dc in next dc) twice: 26 dc and 20 ch-2 sps.

Row 4: Ch 3 (**counts as first dc**), turn; 2 dc in first dc, ch 2, skip next ch-2 sp, sc in next ch-2 sp, ch 5, sc in next ch-2 sp, ch 2, ★ skip next ch-2 sp, 5 dc in next dc, ch 2, skip next ch-2 sp, sc in next ch-2 sp, ch 5, sc in next ch-2 sp, ch 2; repeat from ★ across to last ch-2 sp, skip last ch-2 sp, 3 dc in last dc: 36 sts and 15 sps.

Row 5: Ch 4, turn; dc in next dc, ch 1, dc in next dc, ch 2, skip next ch-2 sp, sc in next ch-5 sp, ch 2, skip next ch-2 sp, dc in next dc, ★ (ch 1, dc in next dc) 4 times, ch 2, skip next ch-2 sp, sc in next ch-5 sp, ch 2, skip next ch-2 sp, dc in next dc; repeat from ★ across to last 2 dc, (ch 1, dc in next dc) twice: 31 sts and 30 sps.

Rows 6-42: Repeat Rows 3-5, 12 times; then repeat Row 3 once **more**: 26 dc and 20 ch-2 sps.

SECOND HALF

Row 1: With **wrong** side facing and 📹 working in free loops of beginning ch *(Fig. 1, page 39)*, 📹 join yarn with dc in first ch *(see Joining With Dc, page 39)*; 2 dc in same ch, ch 2, skip next 3 chs, sc in next ch, ch 5, skip next 3 chs, sc in next ch, ★ ch 2, skip next 3 chs, 5 dc in next ch, ch 2, skip next 3 chs, sc in next ch, ch 5, skip next 3 chs, sc in next ch; repeat from ★ across to within 3 chs of marked ch, ch 2, skip next 3 chs, 3 dc in marked ch: 36 sts and 15 sps.

Rows 2-42: Repeat Rows 2-42 of First Half: 26 dc and 20 ch-2 sps.

Do **not** finish off.

EDGING

Rnd 1 (Right side)**:** Ch 2 (**counts as first hdc**), do **not** turn; working in end of rows, 2 hdc in first row, † 2 hdc in next row and in each row across to last row, 3 hdc in last row; working in sts across Row 42, (ch 3, skip next ch-2 sp, sc in next dc) twice, 📹 sc in sp **before** next dc *(Fig. 2, page 39)*, sc in next dc, ★ ch 3, skip next ch-2 sp, sc in next dc, (ch 4, skip next ch-2 sp, sc in next dc) twice, ch 3, skip next ch-2 sp, sc in next dc, sc in sp **before** next dc and in next dc; repeat from ★ 3 times **more**, ch 3, skip next ch-2 sp, sc in next dc, ch 3, skip last ch-2 sp and last dc †; working in end of rows, 3 hdc in first row, repeat from † to † once; join with slip st to first hdc: 398 sts and 40 sps.

Rnd 2: Ch 1, 3 sc in same st, † sc in each hdc across to within one hdc of next ch-3 sp, 3 sc in next hdc and in next ch-3 sp, sc in next sc, 3 sc in next ch-3 sp, skip next sc, sc in next sc, skip next sc, 3 sc in next ch-3 sp, sc in next sc, ★ 5 sc in next ch-4 sp, (sc, ch 4, sc) in next sc, 5 sc in next ch-4 sp, sc in next sc, 3 sc in next ch-3 sp, skip next sc, sc in next sc, skip next sc, 3 sc in next ch-3 sp, sc in next sc; repeat from ★ 3 times **more** †, 3 sc in next ch-3 sp and in next hdc, repeat from † to † once, 3 sc in last ch-3 sp; join with slip st to first sc.

Rnd 3: ★ Slip st **loosely** in next sc and in each sc across to next ch-4 sp, 5 sc in next ch-4 sp; repeat from ★ 7 times **more**, slip st **loosely** in each sc across; join with slip st to first slip st, finish off.

diamonds

Approximate Finished Size:

17" high x 67" wide (43 cm x 170 cm) including fringe

SHOPPING LIST

Yarn (Medium Weight)

[3.5 ounces, 170 yards

(100 grams, 156 meters) per skein]:

☐ 4 skeins

Crochet Hook

☐ Size K (6.5 mm) **or** size needed for gauge

GAUGE INFORMATION

In pattern, 2 repeats = 5¼" (13.25 cm);

6 rows = 4" (10 cm)

Gauge Swatch: 5½" wide x 4" high

(14 cm x 10 cm)

Ch 18.

Work same as First Half for 6 rows: 14 dc and 10 ch-1 sps.

Finish off.

INSTRUCTIONS

FIRST HALF

Ch 50.

Row 1 (Right side)**:** Sc in second ch from hook, ★ ch 3, skip next 3 chs, 3 dc in next ch, ch 3, skip next 3 chs, sc in next ch; repeat from ★ across: 25 sts and 12 ch-3 sps.

Note: Loop a short piece of yarn around any stitch to mark Row 1 as **right** side.

Row 2: Ch 3 (**counts as first dc**), turn; skip next ch-3 sp, (dc, ch 1, dc) in next dc, (ch 1, dc) twice in each of next 2 dc, ★ skip next 2 ch-3 sps, (dc, ch 1, dc) in next dc, (ch 1, dc) twice in each of next 2 dc; repeat from ★ across to last ch-3 sp, skip last ch-3 sp, dc in last sc: 38 dc and 30 ch-1 sps.

Row 3: Ch 1, turn; sc in first dc, ch 3, skip next 2 ch-1 sps, 3 dc in next ch-1 sp, ★ ch 3, skip next 2 ch-1 sps and next dc, sc in sp **before** next dc (*Fig. 2, page 39*), ch 3, skip next 2 ch-1 sps, 3 dc in next ch-1 sp; repeat from ★ across to last 2 ch-1 sps, ch 3, skip last 2 ch-1 sps and next dc, sc in last dc: 25 sts and 12 ch-3 sps.

Rows 4-45: Repeat Rows 2 and 3, 21 times: 25 sts and 12 ch-3 sps.

Finish off.

SECOND HALF

Row 1: With **right** side facing and working in free loops of beginning ch (*Fig. 1, page 39*), join yarn with sc in first ch (*see Joining With Sc, page 39*); ★ ch 3, skip next 3 chs, 3 dc in next ch, ch 3, skip next 3 chs, sc in next ch; repeat from ★ across: 25 sts and 12 ch-3 sps.

Rows 2-45: Repeat Rows 2-45 of First Half: 25 sts and 12 ch-3 sps.

Do **not** finish off.

EDGING

Rnd 1 (Right side)**:** Ch 2 (**counts as first hdc**), do **not** turn; working in end of rows, skip first sc row, † (3 hdc in next dc row, skip next sc row) 22 times, hdc in beginning ch, (skip next sc row, 3 hdc in next dc row) 22 times, hdc in last sc row; working in sts and sps across Row 45 of next Half, 5 hdc in next ch-3 sp, hdc in next 3 dc, (3 hdc in next ch-3 sp, hdc in next sc, 3 hdc in next ch-3 sp, hdc in next 3 dc) across to last ch-3 sp, 5 hdc in last ch-3 sp †; working in end of rows, hdc in first sc row, repeat from † to † once; join with slip st to first hdc: 396 hdc.

Rnd 2: Slip st **loosely** in next 136 hdc, † sc in next hdc, (ch 23, sc in next 2 hdc) 28 times, (ch 23, sc in next hdc) twice †, slip st **loosely** in next 139 hdc, repeat from † to † once, slip st in last 3 hdc; join with slip st to first slip st, finish off.

elegance

Approximate Finished Size:

17½" high x 62½" wide (44.5 cm x 159 cm)

SHOPPING LIST

Yarn (Medium Weight)

[3.5 ounces, 170 yards

(100 grams, 156 meters) per skein]:

☐ 4 skeins

Crochet Hook

☐ Size K (6.5 mm) **or** size needed for gauge

GAUGE INFORMATION

In pattern, 2 repeats = 5½" (14 cm);

 4 rows = 1⅞" (4.75 cm)

Gauge Swatch: 5¾" wide x 3¾" high

 (14.5 cm x 9.5 cm)

Ch 18.

Work same as First Half for 8 rows: 7 sc and 6 ch-3 sps.

Finish off.

─────── **STITCH GUIDE** ───────

 TREBLE CROCHET (abbreviated tr)

YO twice, insert hook in sp indicated, YO and pull up a loop (4 loops on hook), (YO and draw through 2 loops on hook) 3 times.

INSTRUCTIONS
FIRST HALF

Ch 50.

Row 1 (Right side)**:** Sc in second ch from hook, ★ ch 1, skip next 3 chs, (3 dc, ch 2, 3 dc) in next ch, ch 1, skip next 3 chs, sc in next ch; repeat from ★ across: 43 sts and 18 sps.

Note: Loop a short piece of yarn around any stitch to mark Row 1 as **right** side.

Row 2: Ch 6 **(counts as first dc plus ch 3)**, turn; skip next ch-1 sp, (sc, ch 3) twice in next ch-2 sp, skip next 3 dc and next ch-1 sp, dc in next sc, ★ ch 3, skip next ch-1 sp, (sc, ch 3) twice in next ch-2 sp, skip next 3 dc and next ch-1 sp, dc in next sc; repeat from ★ across: 19 sts and 18 ch-3 sps.

Row 3: Ch 3 (**counts as first hdc plus ch 1**), turn; sc in next ch-3 sp, (ch 3, sc in next ch-3 sp) across to last dc, ch 1, hdc in last dc: 20 sts and 19 sps.

Row 4: Ch 1, turn; sc in first hdc, ch 3, skip next ch-1 sp, (sc in next ch-3 sp, ch 3) across to last ch-1 sp, skip last ch-1 sp, sc in last hdc: 19 sts and 18 ch-3 sps.

Row 5: Ch 1, turn; sc in first sc, ★ ch 1, skip next ch-3 sp, (3 dc, ch 2, 3 dc) in next ch-3 sp, ch 1, skip next ch-3 sp, sc in next sc; repeat from ★ across: 43 sts and 18 sps.

Rows 6-61: Repeat Rows 2-5, 14 times: 43 sts and 18 sps.

Finish off.

SECOND HALF

Row 1: With **right** side facing and 🎥 working in free loops of beginning ch (**Fig. 1, page 39**), 🎥 join yarn with sc in first ch (**see Joining With Sc, page 39**); ★ ch 1, skip next 3 chs, (3 dc, ch 2, 3 dc) in next ch, ch 1, skip next 3 chs, sc in next ch; repeat from ★ across: 43 sts and 18 sps.

Rows 2-61: Repeat Rows 2-61 of First Half: 43 sts and 18 sps.

Do **not** finish off.

EDGING

Rnd 1 (Right side)**:** Ch 2, do **not** turn; ★ working in end of rows, 3 hdc in first row, hdc in next row, 2 hdc in next row, 3 hdc in next row, (hdc in next 2 rows, 2 hdc in next row, 3 hdc in next row) 14 times, 3 dc in next row, tr in beginning ch, 3 dc in next row, 3 hdc in next row, 2 hdc in next row, (hdc in next 2 rows, 2 hdc in next row, 3 hdc in next row) 14 times, hdc in next row, 3 hdc in last row; working in sts across Row 61, hdc in next ch-1 sp, dc in next 3 dc, 3 tr in next ch-2 sp, dc in next 3 dc, hdc in next ch-1 sp, † [(sc, ch 3, slip st in third ch from hook, sc) in next sc (**Picot made**)], hdc in next ch-1 sp, dc in next 3 dc, 3 tr in next ch-2 sp, dc in next 3 dc, hdc in next ch-1 sp †; repeat from † to † 4 times **more**, skip last sc; repeat from ★ once **more**; skip beginning ch-2 and join with slip st to first hdc: 574 sts and 10 Picots.

Rnd 2: Slip st **loosely** in next 109 sts, † slip st in next tr, (ch 4, slip st in third ch from hook) 3 times, ch 1, slip st in same tr, slip st **loosely** in next 115 sts, slip st in next tr, (ch 4, slip st in third ch from hook) 3 times, ch 1, ★ slip st in same tr, slip st **loosely** in next 5 sts, keeping picot to **right** side, skip picot and slip st **loosely** in next 5 sts, slip st in next tr, (ch 4, slip st in third ch from hook) 3 times, ch 1; repeat from ★ 4 times **more**, slip st in same tr †, slip st **loosely** in next 115 sts, repeat from † to † once, slip st **loosely** in last 6 sts; join with slip st to first slip st, finish off.

whimsy

◼◼◻◻ EASY +

Approximate Finished Size:

20" high x 68½" wide (51 cm x 174 cm)

SHOPPING LIST

Yarn (Medium Weight)

[3.5 ounces, 170 yards

(100 grams, 156 meters) per skein]:

☐ 5 skeins

Crochet Hook

☐ Size K (6.5 mm) **or** size needed for gauge

GAUGE INFORMATION

In pattern, (sc, ch 3, 2 dc) 3 times = 3½" (9 cm)

and 6 rows = 3¾" (9.5 cm)

Gauge Swatch: 3¾" square (9.5 cm)

Ch 11.

Work same as First Half for 6 rows: 10 sts and 3 ch-3 sps.

Finish off.

INSTRUCTIONS
FIRST HALF

Ch 44; place a marker in second ch from hook for Second Half placement.

Row 1 (Wrong side)**:** (Sc, ch 3, 2 dc) in second ch from hook, ★ skip next 2 chs, (sc, ch 3, 2 dc) in next ch; repeat from ★ across to last 3 chs, skip next 2 chs, sc in last ch: 43 sts and 14 ch-3 sps.

Note: Loop a short piece of yarn around **back** of any stitch on Row 1 to mark **right** side.

Rows 2-51: Ch 1, turn; (sc, ch 3, 2 dc) in first sc, (sc, ch 3, 2 dc) in next ch-3 sp and in each ch-3 sp across to last ch-3 sp, sc in last ch-3 sp.

Row 52: Ch 1, turn; (sc, ch 3, 2 dc) in first sc, (sc, ch 3, 2 dc) in next ch-3 sp and in each ch-3 sp across, slip st in last sc, finish off: 15 ch-3 sps.

SECOND HALF

Row 1: With **wrong** side facing and 🎥 working in free loops of beginning ch *(Fig. 1, page 39)*, 🎥 join yarn with sc in first ch *(see Joining With Sc, page 39)*; ch 3, 2 dc in same st, ★ skip next 2 chs, (sc, ch 3, 2 dc) in next ch; repeat from ★ across to within 2 chs of marked ch, skip next 2 chs, sc in marked ch: 43 sts and 14 ch-3 sps.

Rows 2-51: Ch 1, turn; (sc, ch 3, 2 dc) in first sc, (sc, ch 3, 2 dc) in next ch-3 sp and in each ch-3 sp across to last ch-3 sp, sc in last ch-3 sp.

Row 52: Ch 1, turn; (sc, ch 3, 2 dc) in first sc, (sc, ch 3, 2 dc) in next ch-3 sp and in each ch-3 sp across, slip st in last sc, do **not** finish off: 15 ch-3 sps.

EDGING

Rnd 1 (Right side)**:** Ch 1, do **not** turn; working in ch-3 sps across end of rows (same sp as sc are worked into), slip st in first ch-3 sp, ch 3 **(counts as first dc)**, 2 dc in same sp, 3 dc in each of next 24 ch-3 sps, † dc in end of next sc, dc in beginning ch and in end of next sc, 3 dc in each of next 25 ch-3 sps, (3 dc, ch 3, 3 dc) in corner ch-3 sp; working in sps across Row 52, 3 dc in each of next 13 ch-3 sps, (3 dc, ch 3, 3 dc) in last ch-3 sp †; working in ch-3 sps across end of rows (same sp as sc are worked into), 3 dc in each of next 25 ch-3 sps, repeat from † to † once; join with slip st to first dc: 408 dc and 4 ch-3 sps.

Rnd 2: Ch 3 **(counts as first hdc plus ch 1)**, ★ skip next dc, (hdc in next dc, ch 1, skip next dc) across to next corner ch-3 sp, (hdc, ch 1) 3 times in corner sp; repeat from ★ around to last 3 dc, skip next dc, hdc in next dc, ch 1, skip last dc; join with slip st to first hdc: 214 hdc and 214 ch-1 sps.

Rnd 3: Slip st in first ch-1 sp, ch 2 **(counts as first hdc)**, 2 hdc in same sp, 3 hdc in next ch-1 sp and in each ch-1 sp around; join with slip st to first hdc: 642 hdc.

Rnd 4: Working from **left** to **right**, 🎥 slip st in sp **before** next hdc *(Fig. 2, page 39)*, 🎥 work reverse hdc in same sp *(Figs. 3a-d, page 39)*, ch 1, skip next 2 hdc, ★ work reverse hdc in sp **before** next hdc, ch 1, skip next 2 hdc; repeat from ★ around; join with slip st to first st, finish off.

togetherness

Shown on page 37.

 EASY

Approximate Finished Size:

18" high x 61" wide (45.5 cm x 155 cm)

SHOPPING LIST

Yarn (Medium Weight) 4

[3.5 ounces, 170 yards

(100 grams, 156 meters) per skein]:

☐ Dk Red - 3 skeins

☐ White - 3 skeins

Crochet Hook

☐ Size J (6 mm) **or** size needed for gauge

GAUGE INFORMATION

In pattern, 2 repeats = 4" (10 cm);

8 rows = 4¼" (10.75 cm)

Gauge Swatch: 4" wide x 3¾" high

(10 cm x 9.5 cm)

With Dk Red, ch 20.

Work same as First Half for 7 rows: 13 sts.

STITCH GUIDE

DOUBLE CROCHET 5 TOGETHER *(abbreviated dc5tog)*

(uses next 5 sts)

★ YO, insert hook in **next** st, YO and pull up a loop, YO and draw through 2 loops on hook; repeat from ★ 4 times **more**, YO and draw through all 6 loops on hook.

INSTRUCTIONS
FIRST HALF

With Dk Red, ch 244; place a marker in fourth ch from hook for Second Half placement.

Row 1 (Right side)**:** 2 Dc in fourth ch from hook (**3 skipped chs count as first dc**), skip next 3 chs, sc in next ch, ★ skip next 3 chs, 5 dc in next ch, skip next 3 chs, sc in next ch; repeat from ★ across to last 4 chs, skip next 3 chs, 3 dc in last ch; finish off: 181 sts.

Note: Loop a short piece of yarn around any stitch to mark Row 1 as **right** side.

Row 2: With **wrong** side facing, 🎥 join White with sc in first dc *(see Joining With Sc, page 39)*; ★ ch 3, dc5tog, ch 3, sc in next dc; repeat from ★ across: 61 sts and 60 ch-3 sps.

Row 3: Ch 3 **(counts as first dc, now and throughout)**, turn; 2 dc in first sc, skip next ch-3 sp, sc in next st, ★ skip next ch-3 sp, 5 dc in next sc, skip next ch-3 sp, sc in next st; repeat from ★ across to last ch-3 sp, skip last ch-3 sp, 3 dc in last sc; finish off: 181 sts.

Row 4: With **wrong** side facing, join Dk Red with sc in first dc; ★ ch 3, dc5tog, ch 3, sc in next dc; repeat from ★ across: 61 sts and 60 ch-3 sps.

Row 5: Ch 3, turn; 2 dc in first sc, skip next ch-3 sp, sc in next st, ★ skip next ch-3 sp, 5 dc in next sc, skip next ch-3 sp, sc in next st; repeat from ★ across to last ch-3 sp, skip last ch-3 sp, 3 dc in last sc; finish off: 181 sts.

Rows 6-17: Repeat Rows 2-5, 3 times: 181 sts.

SECOND HALF

Row 1: With **right** side facing and 🎥 working in free loops of beginning ch *(Fig. 1, page 39)*, 🎥 join Dk Red with dc in first ch *(see Joining With Dc, page 39)*; 2 dc in same st, skip next 3 chs, sc in next ch, ★ skip next 3 chs, 5 dc in next ch, skip next 3 chs, sc in next ch; repeat from ★ across to within 3 chs of marked ch, skip next 3 chs, 3 dc in marked ch; finish off: 181 sts.

Rows 2-17: Repeat Rows 2-17 of First Half: 181 sts.

Do **not** finish off.

EDGING

Rnd 1 (Right side): Do **not** turn; slip st in end of first row, ch 3; dc evenly across end of rows, ch 3; slip st **loosely** in each st across Row 17, ch 3; dc evenly across end of rows, ch 3; slip st **loosely** in each st across Row 17, ch 3; join with slip st to first dc, finish off.

general instructions

ABBREVIATIONS

ch(s)	chain(s)
cm	centimeters
dc	double crochet(s)
dc3tog	double crochet 3 together
dc5tog	double crochet 5 together
dtr	double treble crochet(s)
hdc	half double crochet(s)
mm	millimeters
Rnd(s)	Round(s)
sc	single crochet(s)
sp(s)	space(s)
st(s)	stitch(es)
tr	treble crochet(s)
YO	yarn over

SYMBOLS & TERMS

★ — work instructions following ★ as many **more** times as indicated in addition to the first time.

† to † or ♥ to ♥ — work all instructions from first † to second † or from first ♥ to second ♥ **as many** times as specified.

( ) or [ ] — work enclosed instructions **as many** times as specified by the number immediately following **or** work all enclosed instructions in the stitch or space indicated **or** contains explanatory remarks.

colon (:) — the number(s) given after a colon at the end of a row or round denote(s) the number of stitches or spaces you should have on that row or round.

CROCHET TERMINOLOGY

UNITED STATES		INTERNATIONAL
slip stitch (slip st)	=	single crochet (sc)
single crochet (sc)	=	double crochet (dc)
half double crochet (hdc)	=	half treble crochet (htr)
double crochet (dc)	=	treble crochet(tr)
treble crochet (tr)	=	double treble crochet (dtr)
double treble crochet (dtr)	=	triple treble crochet (ttr)
triple treble crochet (tr tr)	=	quadruple treble crochet (qtr)
skip	=	miss

Yarn Weight Symbol & Names	LACE 0	SUPER FINE 1	FINE 2	LIGHT 3	MEDIUM 4	BULKY 5	SUPER BULKY 6
Type of Yarns in Category	Fingering, 10-count crochet thread	Sock, Fingering Baby	Sport, Baby	DK, Light Worsted	Worsted, Afghan, Aran	Chunky, Craft, Rug	Bulky, Roving
Crochet Gauge* Ranges in Single Crochet to 4" (10 cm)	32-42 double crochets**	21-32 sts	16-20 sts	12-17 sts	11-14 sts	8-11 sts	5-9 sts
Advised Hook Size Range	Steel*** 6,7,8 Regular hook B-1	B-1 to E-4	E-4 to 7	7 to I-9	I-9 to K-10.5	K-10.5 to M-13	M-13 and larger

*GUIDELINES ONLY: The chart above reflects the most commonly used gauges and hook sizes for specific yarn categories.

** Lace weight yarns are usually crocheted on larger-size hooks to create lacy openwork patterns. Accordingly, a gauge range is difficult to determine. Always follow the gauge stated in your pattern.

*** Steel crochet hooks are sized differently from regular hooks–the higher the number the smaller the hook, which is the reverse of regular hook sizing.

CROCHET HOOKS																
U.S.	B-1	C-2	D-3	E-4	F-5	G-6	H-8	I-9	J-10	K-10½	L-11	M/N-13	N/P-15	P/Q	Q	S
Metric - mm	2.25	2.75	3.25	3.5	3.75	4	5	5.5	6	6.5	8	9	10	15	16	19

■□□□ BEGINNER	Projects for first-time crocheters using basic stitches. Minimal shaping.
■■□□ EASY	Projects using yarn with basic stitches, repetitive stitch patterns, simple color changes, and simple shaping and finishing.
■■■□ INTERMEDIATE	Projects using a variety of techniques, such as basic lace patterns or color patterns, mid-level shaping and finishing.
■■■■ EXPERIENCED	Projects with intricate stitch patterns, techniques and dimension, such as non-repeating patterns, multi-color techniques, fine threads, small hooks, detailed shaping and refined finishing.

GAUGE

Exact gauge is **essential** for proper size. Before beginning your Shawl, make the sample swatch given in the individual instructions in the yarn and hook specified. After completing the swatch, measure it, counting your stitches and rows carefully. If your swatch is larger or smaller than specified, **make another, changing hook size to get the correct gauge.**

JOINING WITH SC

When instructed to join with a sc, begin with a slip knot on the hook. Insert the hook in the stitch or space indicated, YO and pull up a loop, YO and draw through both loops on the hook.

JOINING WITH HDC

When instructed to join with a hdc, begin with a slip knot on the hook. YO, holding the loop on the hook, insert the hook in the stitch or space indicated, YO and pull up a loop, YO and draw through all 3 loops on the hook.

JOINING WITH DC

When instructed to join with a dc, begin with a slip knot on the hook. YO, holding the loop on the hook, insert the hook in the stitch or space indicated, YO and pull up a loop (3 loops on hook), (YO and draw through 2 loops on hook) twice.

FREE LOOPS OF A CHAIN

When instructed to work in free loops of a chain, work in loop indicated by arrow (Fig. 1).

Fig. 1

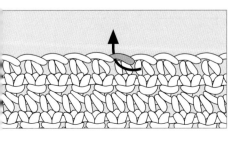

WORKING IN A SPACE BEFORE A STITCH

When instructed to work in a space **before** a stitch or in spaces **between** stitches, insert the hook in the space indicated by arrow (Fig. 2).

Fig. 2

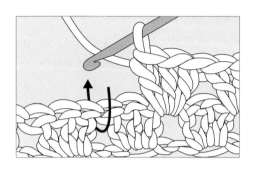

REVERSE HALF DOUBLE CROCHET
(abbreviated reverse hdc)

Working from **left** to **right**, YO, insert hook in st or sp indicated to right of hook (Fig. 3a), YO and draw through, under and to left of loops on hook (3 loops on hook) (Fig. 3b), YO and draw through all 3 loops on hook (Fig. 3c) (reverse hdc made, Fig. 3d).

Fig. 3a

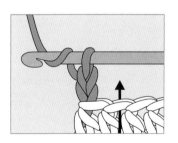

Fig. 3b

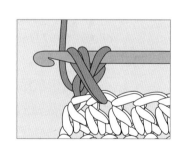

Fig. 3c

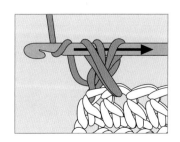

Fig. 3d

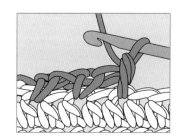

yarn information

Each Shawl in this book was made using Medium Weight Yarn. Any brand of Medium Weight Yarn may be used. It is best to refer to the yardage/meters when determining how many balls or skeins to purchase. Remember, to arrive at the finished size, it is the GAUGE/TENSION that is important, not the brand of yarn. For your convenience, listed below are the specific yarns used to create our photography models.

STATUESQUE
Lion Brand® Vanna's Choice®
#401 Grey Marble

ZESTY
Lion Brand® Vanna's Choice®
Orange - #134 Terracotta
Burnt Orange - #133 Brick

CHARMING
Lion Brand® Vanna's Choice®
Green - #173 Dusty Green
Lion Brand® Vanna's Choice® Baby
Yellow - #157 Duckie

PASSIONATE
Lion Brand® Vanna's Choice®
#113 Scarlet

FROLIC
Lion Brand® Vanna's Choice®
#301 Rose Mist

COZY
Lion Brand® Vanna's Choice®
Lt Green - #304 Seaspray Mist
Green - #171 Fern
Dk Green - #172 Kelly Green

ROMANCE
Lion Brand® Vanna's Choice®
#144 Magenta

JOY
Lion Brand® Vanna's Choice®
#100 White

DIAMONDS
Lion Brand® Vanna's Choice®
#123 Beige

ELEGANCE
Lion Brand® Vanna's Choice®
#153 Black

WHIMSY
Lion Brand® Vanna's Choice® Baby
#157 Duckie

TOGETHERNESS
Lion Brand® Vanna's Choice®
Dk Red - #180 Cranberry
White - #100 White

We have made every effort to ensure that these instructions are accurate and complete. We cannot, however, be responsible for human error, typographical mistakes, or variations in individual work.

Production Team: Writer/Technical Editor - Linda A. Daley; Editorial Writers - Susan McManus Johnson and Susan Frantz Wiles; Senior Graphic Artist - Lora Puls; Graphic Designers: Dana Vaughn and Becca Snider Tally; Photo Stylist - Brook Duszota; and Photographer - Jason Masters.